The Elephant and the Black Cobra

ANIMAL SHORT STORIES

Contents

Rikki-Tikki-Tavi 3
by Rudyard Kipling
illustrated by Matthew Williams

The Underwater Elephants 18
by Linda Newbery
illustrated by Merrick Durling

Brown Hare and the Fox 34
by Martin Waddell
illustrated by Caroline Sharpe

The Underwater Elephants © Linda Newbery 2003
Brown Hare and the Fox © Martin Waddell 2003
Series editors: Martin Coles and Christine Hall

PEARSON EDUCATION LIMITED
Edinburgh Gate
Harlow
Essex CM20 2JE
England

www.longman.co.uk

The right of Rudyard Kipling, Linda Newbery and Martin Waddell to be identified as the authors of this work has been asserted by them in accordance with the Copyright, Designs and Patents Act, 1988.

We are grateful to A.P Watt Ltd on behalf of The National Trust for Places of Historical Interest or Natural Beauty for permission to reproduce *Rikki-Tikki-Tavi* from *The Jungle Book* by Rudyard Kipling.

All rights reserved. No part of this publication may be reproduced, stored in a retrieval system, or transmitted in any form or by any means, electronic, mechanical, photocopying, recording, or otherwise without either the prior written permission of the Publishers or a licence permitting restricted copying in the United Kingdom issued by the Copyright Licensing Agency Ltd, 90 Tottenham Court Road, London W1P 9HE.

First published 2003
ISBN 0582 79608 3

Illustrated by Matthew Williams (The Organisation), Merrick Durling (SGA) and Caroline Sharpe (Heather Richards)

Printed in Great Britain by Scotprint, Haddington

The publishers' policy is to use paper manufactured from sustainable forests.

Rikki-Tikki-Tavi
by Rudyard Kipling

This is the story of the great war that Rikki-tikki-tavi fought single-handed, through the bath-rooms of the big bungalow in Segowlee. Darzee, the tailor-bird, helped him, but Rikki-tikki did the real fighting.

He was a mongoose, rather like a little cat in his fur and his tail, but quite like a weasel in his head and habits. His eyes and the end of his nose were pink; he could scratch himself anywhere he pleased, with any leg, front or back. He could fluff up his tail, and his war-cry, as he scuttled through the long grass, was: "*Rikk-tikk-tikki-tikki-tchk!*"

One day, a flood washed him out of the burrow where he lived with his father and mother, and carried him down a ditch.

He found a little wisp of grass and clung to it till he lost his senses. When he revived, he was lying in the hot sun on the middle of a garden path and a small boy was saying: "Here's a dead mongoose. Let's have a funeral."

"No," said his mother; "let's take him in and dry him. Perhaps he isn't really dead."

They took him into the house, and a big man picked him up, wrapped him in cotton-wool, and warmed him and he opened his eyes and sneezed.

"Now," said the big man "don't frighten him and we'll see what he'll do."

It is the hardest thing in the world to frighten a mongoose. The motto of all the mongoose family is 'Run and find out'; and Rikki-tikki was a true mongoose. He looked at the cotton-wool, decided that it was not good to eat, ran all round the table, sat up, scratched himself, and jumped on the small boy's shoulder.

"Don't be frightened, Teddy," said his father. "That's his way of making friends."

"Ouch! He's tickling under my chin," said Teddy.

Rikki-tikki snuffed at his ear, and climbed down to the floor, where he sat rubbing his nose.

"Good gracious," said Teddy's mother, "and that's a wild creature! I suppose he's so tame because we've been kind to him."

"All mongooses are like that," said her husband. "If Teddy doesn't pick him up by the tail, or try to put him in a cage, he'll run in and out of the house all day long. Let's give him something to eat."

They gave him a little piece of raw meat. Rikki-tikki liked it, and when it was finished he sat in the sunshine and fluffed up his fur to make it dry. Then he felt better.

"There are more things to find out about in this house," he said to himself, "I shall stay and find out."

He spent all that day roaming over the house. He nearly drowned himself in the bath tubs, put his nose into the ink on a writing-table, and burnt it on the end of the big man's cigar. At nightfall he ran into Teddy's nursery to watch how the lamps were lighted, and when Teddy went to bed Rikki-tikki climbed up too. Teddy's mother and father came in and Rikki-tikki was awake on the pillow. "I don't like that," said Teddy's mother; "he may bite the child."

"He'll do no such thing," said the father. "Teddy's safer with that little beast than if he had a bloodhound to watch him. If a snake came into the nursery now –"

But Teddy's mother wouldn't think of anything so awful.

Early in the morning Rikki-tikki came to breakfast riding on Teddy's shoulder, and they gave him banana and some boiled egg.

Then Rikki-tikki went out into the garden to see what was to be seen. Rikki-tikki licked his lips. "This is a splendid hunting-ground," he said and he scuttled up and down the garden, snuffing here and there till he heard very sorrowful voices in a thorn-bush.

It was Darzee, the tailor-bird, and his wife. Their nest swayed as they sat on the rim and cried.

"What is the matter?" asked Rikki-tikki.

"We are very miserable," said Darzee. "One of our babies fell out of the nest yesterday, and Nag ate him."

"H'm!" said Rikki-tikki, "that is very sad – but I am a stranger here. Who is Nag?"

From the thick grass at the foot of the bush there came a low hiss – a horrid cold sound that made Rikki-tikki jump back. Then out of the grass rose up the head and spread hood of Nag, the big black cobra, and he was five feet long from tongue to tail. He looked at Rikki-tikki with the wicked snake's eyes that never change their expression, whatever the snake may be thinking of.

"Who is Nag?" said he. "I am Nag. Look, and be afraid!"

Rikki-tikki was afraid for the minute; but it is impossible for a mongoose to stay frightened for any length of time. And though Rikki-tikki had never met a live cobra before, his mother had fed him on dead ones, and he knew that all a grown mongoose's business in life was to fight and eat snakes. Nag knew that too, and at the bottom of his cold heart he was afraid.

"Well," said Rikki-tikki, "do you think it is right for you to eat fledglings out of a nest?"

Nag was thinking to himself. He knew that mongooses in the garden meant death sooner or later for him and his family, but he wanted to get Rikki-tikki off his guard. So he dropped his head a little, and put it on one side.

"Let us talk," he said. "You eat eggs. Why should not I eat birds?"

"Behind you! Look behind you!" sang Darzee.

Rikki-tikki jumped up in the air as high as he could go, and just under him whizzed by the head of Nagaina, Nag's wicked wife. She had crept up behind him as he was talking, to make an end of him. He came down almost across her back. He bit, but did not bite long enough, and he jumped

fledglings: young birds

clear of the whisking tail, leaving Nagaina torn and angry.

Rikki-tikki felt his eyes growing red and hot (when a mongoose's eyes grow red, he is angry), and he sat back on his tail and chattered with rage. But Nag and Nagaina had disappeared into the grass. When a snake misses its stroke, it never says anything or gives any sign of what it means to do next. Rikki-tikki did not care to follow them, for he did not feel sure that he could manage two snakes at once. So he trotted off to the path near the house, and sat down to think. It was a serious matter for him.

When Teddy came running down the path, Rikki-tikki was ready to be petted.

But just as Teddy was stooping a tiny voice said: "Be careful. I am death!" It was Karait, the dusty brown snakeling that lies on the dusty earth; and his bite is as dangerous as the cobra's. But he is so small that nobody thinks of him, and so he does more harm to people.

Rikki-tikki's eyes grew red again, and he danced up to Karait with the rocking, swaying motion that he had inherited from his family. If Rikki-tikki had only known, he was doing a much more dangerous thing than fighting Nag, for Karait is so small, and can turn so quickly, that unless Rikki bit him close to the back of the head, he would get the return-stroke in his eye or lip. But Rikki did not know: his eyes were all red, and he rocked back and forth, looking for a good place to hold. Karait struck out. Rikki jumped sideways and tried to run forward, but the wicked little dusty gray head lashed and he had to jump over the body.

Teddy shouted to the house: "Oh, look here! Our mongoose is killing a snake"; and Rikki-tikki heard a scream from Teddy's mother. His father ran out with a stick, but by the time he came up, Rikki-tikki had sprung, jumped on the snake's back, bitten as high up the back as he could get hold, and rolled away. Rikki-tikki was just going to eat him up from the tail, when he remembered that a full meal makes a slow mongoose, and if he wanted all his strength and quickness ready, he must keep himself thin.

He went away for a dust-bath under the bushes, while Teddy's father beat the dead Karait. "What is the use of that?" thought Rikki-tikki. "I have settled it all". Then Teddy's mother picked him up from the dust and hugged him, crying that he had saved Teddy from death, and Teddy looked on with big scared eyes. Rikki-tikki was enjoying himself.

That night, at dinner, walking among the glasses on the table, he could have stuffed himself three times over with nice things; but he remembered Nag and Nagaina, and his eyes would get red, and he would go off into his long war-cry of "*Rikk-tikk-tikki-tikki-tchk!*"

Teddy carried him off to bed, but as soon as Teddy was asleep he went off for his nightly walk round the house.

Rikki-tikki listened. The house was as still as still, but he thought he could just catch the faintest *scratch-scratch*.

"That's Nag or Nagaina," he said to himself; "and he's crawling into the bath-room". He stole off to Teddy's bath-room, and he heard Nag and Nagaina whispering together outside.

"Go in quietly," said Nagaina to her husband, "and remember that the big man who killed Karait is the first one to bite. Then come out and tell me, and we will hunt for Rikki-tikki together."

"But are you sure that there is anything to be gained by killing the people?" said Nag.

"Everything. When there were no people in the bungalow, did we have any mongoose in the garden? So long as the bungalow is empty, we are king and queen of the garden; and remember that as soon as our eggs hatch, our children will need room and quiet."

"I had not thought of that," said Nag. "I will go. I will kill the big man and his wife, and the child if I can, and come away quietly. Then the bungalow will be empty, and Rikki-tikki will go."

Rikki-tikki tingled all over with rage and hatred at this, and then Nag's head appeared, and his five feet of cold body followed it.

Rikki-tikki was very frightened as he saw the size of the big cobra. Nag coiled himself down, coil by coil, round the bottom of the water-jar, and Rikki-tikki stayed still as death.

After an hour he began to move toward the jar. Nag was asleep, and Rikki-tikki looked at his big back. "If I don't break his back at the first jump," said Rikki, "he can still fight; and if he fights – O Rikki!"

"It must be the head," he said "and when I am there, I must not let go."

Then he jumped. The head was lying a little clear of the water-jar; and, as his teeth met, Rikki braced his back to hold down the head. Then he was battered to and fro as a rat is shaken by a dog – to and fro on the floor, up and down, and round in great circles; but his eyes were red, and he held on. As he held he closed his jaws tighter and tighter, for he was sure he would be banged to death.

He was dizzy and felt shaken to pieces when something went off like a thunderclap just behind him; a hot wind knocked him senseless, and red fire singed his fur. The big man had fired both barrels of a shot-gun into Nag.

Rikki-tikki held on with his eyes shut, for now he was quite sure he was dead; but the head did not move, and the big man picked him up and said: "It's the mongoose again, Alice; the little chap has saved *our* lives now." Then Teddy's mother came in with a very white face, and saw what was left of Nag, and Rikki-tikki dragged himself to Teddy's bedroom.

When morning came he was very stiff, but well pleased with his doings.

Without waiting for breakfast, Rikki-tikki ran to the thorn-bush where Darzee was singing a song at the top of his voice. The news of Nag's death was all over the garden.

"Nag is dead – is dead – is dead!" sang Darzee. "Rikki-tikki caught him by the head and held fast. The big man brought the bang-stick, and Nag fell in two pieces! He will never eat my babies again."

The Underwater Elephants
by Linda Newbery

You've probably wondered why elephants have such long noses.

Have they always had them?

Don't they get in the way?

The answer is simple. Elephants' trunks are breathing tubes. Long ago, when rivers were deep and wide, elephants lived underwater.

Not many people know that. But you do.

* * * * *

When Mango was a baby, she and her family lived in a deep river. While the sun baked the land on long summer days, the elephant family stayed in the water, with just the tips of their trunks showing. If you walked along the riverbank – but no-one ever did – all you'd see would be the tips of elephant trunks, from Gumbo's, the biggest, down to Mango's, the smallest. You'd have thought, "What are those? Plants? Fish?"

The older elephants could stay like that for hours, quite still. When they got hungry, they'd reach up to the river-bank for some grass.

For Mango and her cousin Rollo, the river was an adventure playground. They could play chase, and hide-and-seek in the weeds, and loop-the-loop.

(What stroke did they swim? Ellie-paddle!)

When they got tired, they could hang below the surface with the grown-ups, enjoying the brush of fish against their soft skin. (Oh, yes. Elephants had soft skin, then. It was only later, when they had to leave the water, that their skins got tough and cracked.)

Mango liked to rest upside-down, with all four feet flat on the surface. She daydreamed as she floated. Sometimes a frog sat on one of

Mango's feet. That tickled, and made her giggle and splutter and turn right way up.

The elephants would have stayed in their underwater world forever – swimming, eating, playing.

But then two things happened.

The first was that the weather got hotter and hotter and the river got shallower.

And the second thing was crocodiles.

* * * * *

At first, crocodiles weren't much bother. There weren't many and they weren't very big.

THE UNDERWATER ELEPHANTS

If an elephant and a crocodile met in the water, they were polite to each other. The river was big and there was plenty of room for everyone.

But the warm water and the food suited the crocodiles. The young crocodiles grew big, with long sharp teeth. And the more crocodiles there were, the bossier they became. You'd have thought they owned the river.

Billow, Mango's mother, showed her how to see off a small crocodile. With the tip of her trunk she tickled its soft tummy. An elephant's trunk is the perfect tickler! Soon the croc was laughing so much that it had to crawl out of the river to rest on the bank.

But there was one crocodile called Sneaker who couldn't be tickled. He liked to sneak up on the elephants from behind. He would grab Mango's tail in his jaws and hang on to it, no matter how fast she swam away. It began as a game. But when a young elephant called Wallow was alone in the river,

Sneaker sneaked up behind and bit off his tail altogether. Snap! And poor Wallow was left with a stump. The croc swam away, grinning, with the end of Wallow's tail dangling from his teeth.

Wallow hoped his tail would grow back, but it never did.

Sneaker had acted very sneakily, Mango thought. Games were all very well – chewing off tails just wasn't fair!

But it was no use trying to explain fairness to Sneaker. He'd give one of his looks and glide into the river without even a splash.

Soon, Mango had a chance to get her own back. *Two* chances.

Even a crocodile has to sleep sometimes, and when she saw Sneaker curled up on the riverbank she crept up to him.

"Never trust a crocodile," Billow had told her. "They often *pretend* to be asleep."

Mango felt sure Sneaker wasn't pretending. She took a deep breath and trumpeted into his ear with all her might.

Sneaker was so startled, he nearly tied himself in a knot! When he saw it was only Mango, he glared at her and snapped his teeth.

Two days later, Mango did something even more silly. While Rollo and Wallow were playing loop-the-loop, she swam off alone, far from the herd.

This was risky, she knew. You never knew who you might meet.

But the water was cool, and the weed was green, and every time Mango reached a bend, she thought, "Just a little bit farther."

And –

THE ELEPHANT, THE HARE AND THE BLACK COBRA

"Just a very little bit farther …"

And –

"Just a little way round the next bend, just far enough to see …"

And what she saw was Sneaker.

Sneaker had found a new place to sleep, in wet, oozy mud. His tail was curled round his back feet and he was snoring gently.

She went towards him.

"Do I dare?" Mango thought.

Yes, she did.

In fact she couldn't resist!

She grabbed Sneaker's tail with her trunk. Then she tugged as hard as she could.

Sneaker woke with a snort. His eyes opened, and glared. His teeth snapped.

He snapped at the air, not at Mango, who ran backwards very fast, still pulling round and round in mad circles.

When she was dizzy, she stopped and let go. Sneaker gave a groggy glare, hissed loudly and slithered into his hole.

Mango had frightened herself. She'd better swim back to the others as fast as she could.

Sploshing into the river, she saw a grey head, two sad eyes and two flapping ears. It was Sorrow, her great-aunt.

"Mango, that was very silly," Sorrow said. "We've only got one river and we have to share it with the crocs. You've made Sneaker angry, and that's bad news for all of us. Elephants never forget – but neither do crocodiles."

Sorrow was right. It was war now. Once, Sneaker had been playful – now he was nasty.

Sneaker called all his friends and relations' and they hurried to help him.

The river seemed full of teeth.

The elephants worried about their trunks. One snap – and there would be a very ashamed elephant with no trunk! Losing a tail was bad enough. Losing a trunk would make life very hard indeed.

Gumbo said the older elephants would take turns guarding the family group. Even the biggest crocodile wouldn't dare approach a big elephant; an elephant's tusks could throw a croc right out of the water. With guards, they could play, sleep or float without worrying about snapping teeth.

The other problem was harder to solve.

Each year it rained less than the last, and the river got shallower and shallower. The new babies were small enough to swim, but Mango was bigger now. She and Rollo couldn't find water deeper than their shoulders. They stood with the others, hot and cross, while their skins got tough in the baking sun. They stamped at the water and sprayed themselves using their trunks. It wasn't the same as floating, deep and cool. Sometimes they'd lie down and roll, just to get wet all over.

There must be another river! A deeper river. Mango stared across the plain, across miles and miles of yellow grass, to the forest trees.

"Come on," she whispered to Rollo, when the others were sleeping. "Let's explore."

* * * * *

Mango and Rollo walked slowly through the long grass. The sun beat down and they flapped their ears to keep cool. Insects buzzed around their heads. Mango didn't like it, but she could see the forest and the shade of trees like a dark pool of water.

Three antelopes sprang across the grass. Mango tried to copy them, but she was too heavy. Rollo trumpeted with laughter, then pointed his trunk at two tall, graceful creatures with long necks. They were walking towards the forest edge.

"Giraffes," Mango whispered. Billow had told her about them.

When the giraffes reached the trees, they began to nibble the highest leaves. Their gentle eyes gazed down at the two elephants.

"Leaves!" Rollo said. "I wonder what they taste like?"

Mango stretched up and grasped a trunkful. She put them into her mouth. Delicious! She reached for more.

Later, very nervously, Mango and Rollo approached Gumbo with their idea. Gumbo could be cross. His watery eyes stared.

"That," he said curling his trunk, "is a ridiculous idea, children. Go away and eat grass."

Mango and Rollo turned away, ears drooping. Wise old Sorrow had overheard. "It *is* a good idea," she whispered, "but you know what Gumbo's like. Much too proud to listen. You must make him think he thought of it himself."

Mango and Rollo looked at each other.

Then Mango started planning.

* * * * *

They waited till Gumbo was asleep. Gumbo asleep was a frightening sight. His mud-grey sides were a shuddering mountain. His snores were rumbling thunder.

Mango and Rollo crept close, hardly daring to breathe.

With her trunk, Mango carried a big branch of acacia leaves. She and Rollo had walked all the way back to the forest to fetch it. She held it close to Gumbo's head. She shook it gently so that the leaves rustled, sounding like cool rain.

Rollo made the bird call he had practised – a soft call, like the trickle of a stream.

Mango let the acacia leaves touch Gumbo's skin, like dappled water. "Trees, *trees*," she whispered in his ear. "Elephants need trees."

Gumbo's ear flapped. The tip of his trunk twitched. He curled his trunk to pull off a few acacia leaves, and he chewed them very thoughtfully, still fast asleep.

He slept for two more hours. When he woke Mango and Rollo moved away. Gumbo planted his front feet in the water, then heaved, lurched and stood upright. He looked round at the herd. Then he raised his trunk and trumpeted loudly

"I have made up my mind," he said grandly. "Since we can't live underwater, we'll live under trees. The cool shade will be like water. There is lots of food. We will use our trunks to pick leaves. We'll find forest streams and swamps. It will be the next best thing to living underwater. And," he added looking down the river, "there will be *no crocodiles*."

A floating log twitched and showed its teeth. It smiled nastily. Wallow gave a shudder and moved closer to the herd.

"We'll leave straight away," Gumbo said, "now that my mind's made up."

All the elephants flapped their ears, which is an elephant's way of clapping.

"What a brilliant idea!" said wise old Sorrow.

Gumbo smiled modestly. "It came to me in a dream," he said. "Just like that."

* * * * *

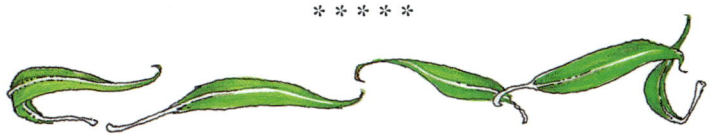

The elephants followed Gumbo into the deep shade of the forest.

Mango turned and lifted her trunk to trumpet a goodbye to Sneaker. "Bet you wish you were coming!" she yelled.

The crocodile watched sadly from the riverbank. He would miss them.

* * * * *

Mango is a wise old elephant now. She has children and grandchildren of her own.

They walk from forest to forest, looking for deep shade and delicious things to eat. They find cool grass to lie on and swamps to wallow in.

But an elephant never forgets, and one of the things an elephant never forgets is where it came from.

If ever you
see a sleeping
elephant, watch it
carefully.

Slowly, it will smile. Its feet will start to paddle. Its trunk will stretch upwards, remembering that it was once a breathing tube.

Then you will know that your elephant is back in the past. It is dreaming of those happy, floating, paddling, wallowing, loop-the-loop days, when elephants lived underwater.

Brown Hare and the Fox
by Martin Waddell

Nora came every year to stay with Grannie Brennan, in the old stone house by the lake.

"I want to go, too," her brother Donal insisted.

"You're not old enough," said his Mammy.

"I am so," said Donal. "I'm nearly six."

That's how Nora wound up looking after one very small brother, which didn't please her at all.

"You're to do what I say!" Nora told Donal.

"Well, maybe I might," grinned small Donal.

Grannie's house was along a stone lane that led to the shore of the lake. Granda's fields ran from the lake, up to the trees that grew on the low slopes of the mountain. Grannie didn't farm

Granda's fields anymore now Granda was dead. The fields were farmed by her neighbour, Jack Rooney.

It was not at all like the city they came from. There were no streets and no cars, and no parks and no shops, and only two houses, Grannie Brennan's and Jack Rooney's.

The grocery van came twice a week down Grannie Brennan's lane, and that's where Grannie Brennan did her shopping. Jack Rooney came over the fields every day to see Grannie. He bought the rest of the stuff that she needed from town.

"A shop in a van?" Donal asked Nora. "Will there be sweets in the van?"

"There'll be sweets," Nora told him.

That pleased Donal, but ...

"Has Grannie Brennan got a TV?" Donal asked.

"There's not much time for TV at Grannie

Brennan's house," Nora said.

That didn't please Donal.

"I'll take you to see old Brown Hare," Nora said, trying to cheer Donal up. "She lives over in Jack Rooney's fields. I saw her the last time I was there."

"What's a hare?" Donal asked.

"You'll see," Nora said. "It's a bit like a very big rabbit."

"I want to see old Brown Hare," Donal told Grannie Brennan that night, as they sat by the fire in her house.

"You'd have to go out in the cold fields at dawn to see her," Grannie said.

"I don't mind that one bit," Donal said … but he *did* mind, next morning.

They had cups of tea in the kitchen, and then they put on their coats and their boots and went out of the house. They went up Granda's fields to the trees, and then they walked to the field above Jack Rooney's house.

Jack's curtains were closed.

"That wise man is still in his bed!" grumbled Grannie.

"He won't see Brown Hare like me!" Donal said.

"He's seen Brown Hare before, many a time," Nora said. "Brown Hare is Jack Rooney's hare."

"Hares belong to no man," Grannie said. "The way a hare thinks, she belongs to herself, and the fields belong to her."

"You'd best not say that to Jack Rooney," said Nora. "He says all these fields are his, not Brown Hare's."

"Does Jack Rooney not like Brown Hare?" Donal asked Grannie.

"She eats the crop from the fields," Grannie said. "Jack Rooney farms for a living. Why should he *like* old Brown Hare?"

They stopped by the black rock, where they could look down at the low fields by the lake.

"Keep very still," Nora told Donal. "Brown Hare has her young ones hidden down there in nests she made for them in the fields. If she thinks we are here, she won't show herself."

"Like birds' nests with eggs?" said Donal.

"They're not eggs," Nora told him. "They are little animals. They're hidden away in places she makes in the grass, or close by the sides of big stones where they can't be seen.

They each have a place of their own, so she won't lose them all if a fox comes and finds one."

"Like burrows and rabbits?" said Donal.

"Not burrows," said Nora. "Just places on top of the ground, or in small dips in the field, or maybe in the reeds round the lake."

"Keep quiet," Grannie said. "You'll scare old Brown Hare."

A cold morning mist hung over the lake.

"I'm bored," Donal said. "Can I go climbing the rock?"

"No you cannot!" Nora hissed.

"But …"

"Hold your wheest!" said old Grannie.

"What's a wheest?" Donal whispered.

"She means, 'Shut up, Donal!'" Nora told him. "It's just one of Grannie's old words."

"Stay still, and wait for Brown Hare to show up," Grannie said.

Donal stayed still. His fingers were cold and so were his feet. His boots were too big. They were an old pair of Grannie's he'd borrowed, because he didn't want to spoil his new trainers in the wet grass.

Then Nora saw something move.

She nudged Grannie and pointed down to the end of Jack Rooney's cow field. There were no cows in the field that morning. Jack Rooney had moved them to fresh grass.

"Something moved!" Nora whispered.

It was Brown Hare.

Brown Hare rose from the hollow in the field, where she'd been hidden. They could see her long back and big ears. She stood stiff backed, with her ears up.

Then she wizzled and twizzled and wrinkled her nose, and she sniffed at the air, and then …

"There goes Brown Hare!" Nora told Donal.
Hoppity-hoppity-hoppity-hop.
Brown Hare stopped.
She wizzled and twizzled and wrinkled her nose, looking round at the field.

"Is that it?" Donal whispered. "Is that all she does?"

"Be quiet!" Nora whispered. "Hares have sharp ears. She can hear a twig snap four fields away."

Hoppity-hoppity-hoppity-hop.

Brown Hare disappeared into a dip in the field, "Can we go home for our breakfast?" Donal asked.

"One of her young ones must be hidden in there," Nora said. "We're staying here till she comes out again."

Donal had lost interest. He was cold and fed up, and his feet were like ice. They stood for what seemed a long time to Donal, but there was no sign of Brown Hare.

"Where is she, Grannie?" asked Nora.

"She's maybe followed the dip and come out in the next field," said Grannie. "If she did we can't see her from here."

"Can we go where we can see her?" asked Nora.

"I want to go home," muttered Donal.

"You're just a nuisance, our Donal," said Nora.

Grannie Brennan and Nora went into the trees above the next field. Donal came trailing behind them. And then …

"Look Nora! Look Donal!" said Grannie. "Look over there two fields away, over there."

Nora looked. At first she saw nothing at all … then she saw something move. "What is it?" asked Nora.

"It's a fox," Grannie said.

"Oh he's lovely," said Nora. "Look Donal."

But Donal was too cold to be bothered looking.

"What's he doing?" asked Nora.

"He'll be searching for Brown Hare's young ones," said Grannie. "He's wanting his breakfast like our Donal is. Donal's breakfast is toast. The fox's breakfast could be our Brown Hare."

"Do foxes eat hares?" Donal said, suddenly interested again, despite the cold.

"Foxes eat anything they can lay hold of," Grannie said. "I'd better be telling Jack Rooney this one is about, so he can mind his chickens."

Nora had gone pale.

The fox was slinking along … now they could see him, now they couldn't. Then …

"Look. Over there!" Nora whispered.

Over there was Brown Hare, two fields away from the fox.

Brown Hare was standing very still, head up in the air. She sniffed at the air.

"She smells fox … but she doesn't know where the fox is," Grannie whispered.

"Run!" Nora said. "Why doesn't she run away?"

"She fears for her young ones," said Grannie. "Watch this now. You'll see what she does. She'll lead him away from her babies."

Red Fox came over the old stone wall, one field away from Brown Hare.

Brown Hare stood upright, with her long ears in the air and her nose twitching.

The fox disappeared in the long grass by the stones, making straight for Brown Hare.

"He knows she is there," whispered Grannie.

"He can't see her," said Donal. "How does the fox know where she is?"

"He has her scent," Grannie said softly. "Look now ... watch Brown Hare."

Brown Hare wizzled and twizzled and wrinkled her nose, and wizzled and twizzled again, and then ...

... she was off.

Hoppity-hoppity-hoppity-hop.

Brown Hare was off, and so was the fox.

Brown Hare twisted and turned as she ran. The fox twisted and turned after Brown Hare.

They ran through one field, and another. Brown Hare turned by the gorse and cut back. Then she stopped by the stone wall between the two fields.

The fox had stopped, too.

"He's lost her," said Donal.

Then the fox moved again, and so did Brown Hare.

She was over the stone wall, and then she turned back and ran over the field, as the fox leaped on top of the wall.

Donal saw the flash of his tail, and the twist of his head as he looked, and then he was after Brown Hare again.

They ran
and they ran
and they ran
and they ran
twisting *this way* and *this way* and *this way* and *that*.

Every turn Brown Hare took, the fox followed.

"Keep running Brown Hare!" Nora called.

The fox and Brown Hare sped over the fields.

Brown Hare turned again and again and again,

this way and *this way* and *this way* and *that*,

that way and *that way* and *that way* and *this* heading back up the fields toward the woods.

"She's coming this way!" Nora shouted.

Brown Hare went by them and into the trees, with the red fox running fast behind her.

The last thing Nora saw was the flash of his tail. "Will he catch her?" asked Nora.

"Will he eat her?" said Donal, looking at Grannie.

"I don't know!" Grannie said. "But that old hare of yours knows her way through the trees. She let him see her ... then she led him away from the places where her young ones were hid. She'll lose the old fox, and then she'll come back to care for her babies."

"If the fox doesn't catch her," said Nora.
"How will we know?" asked Donal.
"Well … we'll come out tonight. We'll watch over the field where her young ones are hidden. If Brown Hare is all right, she will come back and take them somewhere else, where they'll be safe from the fox," Grannie said.

"What if Brown Hare doesn't come?" Nora said.

"Then we'll have cold feet for nothing," said Grannie.

They waited all day, and just after sunset they went out to the fields, wrapped up in their coats and their boots.

And …

The fields were cold and empty. There was no sign of Brown Hare.

The moon rose, and still they waited. Nothing moved in the shadows. The moonlight spread slowly. It made a shiny path over the lake, from one side to the other. The only sound was the soft lap of the water.

"Brown Hare must be dead," Donal said. He'd gone pale. "The old fox has eaten her."

Nora said nothing. There were tears in her eyes. She didn't *want* Brown Hare to be dead.

Then …

"Look there!" Grannie whispered.

It was Brown Hare in the field by the lake.

She wizzled and twizzled and wrinkled her nose, and then she slipped away into the reeds.

"It's all right!" Donal said, hugging Grannie.

Nora just stood there and beamed. She'd no need for tears now.

Brown Hare had escaped from the fox.